Also by August Kleinzahler

SNOW

APPROACHING

ON

THE

HUDSON

AUGUST

KLEINZAHLER

SNOW

APPROACHING

ON

THE

HUDSON

FARRAR STRAUS GIROUX

NEW YORK

Farrar, Straus and Giroux
120 Broadway, New York 10271

Library of Congress Cataloging-in-Publication Data
Names: Kleinzahler, August, author.
Title: Snow approaching on the Hudson : poems / August Kleinzahler.
Description: First edition. | New York : Farrar, Straus and Giroux, 2020.
Identifiers: LCCN 2020013404 | ISBN 9780374266271 (hardcover)
Subjects: LCGFT: Poetry.
Classification: LCC PS3561.L38285 S66 2020 | DDC 811/.54—dc23
LC record available at https://lccn.loc.gov/2020013404

Designed by Crisis

Our books may be purchased in bulk for promotional, educational,
or business use. Please contact your local bookseller or the
Macmillan Corporate and Premium Sales Department at 1-800-221-7945,
extension 5442, or by e-mail at MacmillanSpecialMarkets@macmillan.com.

www.fsgbooks.com
www.twitter.com/fsgbooks
www.facebook.com/fsgbooks

1 3 5 7 9 10 8 6 4 2

TO FRIENDS DEPARTED—

"SEE YOU ON THE RIVER"

CONTENTS

SNOW

APPROACHING

ON

THE

HUDSON

—*Elvis is dead*, the radio said,
where it sat behind a fresh-baked loaf of bread
and broken link of *kolbasz*
fetched only lately from Boucherie Hongroise:
Still Life Without Blue Pitcher.
I read that piece of meat as if I were Chaim Soutine,
with its capillaries and tiny kernels of fat,
bound up in its burnt-sienna casing.
There and then the motif came to me
that would anchor my early masterwork, Opus 113.
No? I'll hum the first few bars.

The window was small,
and set low on the wall. Little out there to see,
only the legs of pedestrians below the knee.
Captive, a prisoner nearly, inside the ochre room,
as the radio poured forth this terrible news:
—*KING ELVIS IS DEAD*
his flesh empurpled, the giant gold medallion,
his lolling tongue bitten nearly in two.

I took note, the time was propitious for soup
even amidst the bulletins and updates, and then made ready
with the preliminary slo-mo casting about that attends
the act of creation,
a length of sausage readily at hand.
Soup-making always seemed to settle me back then.

Those with whom I lived considered me vain,
excepting the Lady M,
with whom I tirelessly played,
Parcheesi, Scrabble, less circumscribed games.
She would have bought for me a giant gold medallion
could she have managed the expense,
if only I would let her.

Presently the soup was the color of the room;
everything around me, the walls, the air,
varying shades of ochre,
but pebbled with paprika-colored nuggets.

They say he existed on Tuinal and cheddar,
his blood turned to sludge,
odds & ends from this snack or that buried deep inside him,
dating all the way back to *Blue Hawaii*,
the fat around his neck like a collar of *boudin blanc*.

Every so often he'd soil his white cape,
and only, it turns out, in Vegas and while on stage.
Now, that's what I call a showman.

Both afternoon and summer were drawing to a close
while the soup thickened on the stove,
the unlit room darkening by degree.
The radio resumed its regular programming,
And, as always seemed the case that hour of the day,
Satie's *Gymnopédies*.

TRAVELER'S TALES /
A HISTORY OF WESTERN
MUSIC: CHAPTER 74

Odd, unsettling somehow, visiting here again after so many
    years,
traveling through town at this hour,
the Baixa nearly deserted, then along the river, the lights of
    the bridge blurred by rain,
just me and the Consul's driver:
customized Citroën C4 Aircross Picasso, outsized
    smoked-glass windows,
upholstered like the inside of a leather queen's crypt,
    brown Bavarian bull hide.
Might as well be in a glass bathyscaphe or slow-motion
    pneumatic tube
forcing its passage through a tunnel of oil.

I mean, how different is this from the last time,
way back when, before our *anthem* hit the charts? It's still
    in everyone's earbuds,
even here: the *fidalgos* in $500 jeans, the Monsignors in
    their black cassocks, purple trim,
the senhora ladling out the *caldo verde* and *feïjoada*.
In those days she would have been dressed in black.
You lived on that kale and potato soup, and with that bottle
    of *piri-piri*

you carried around everywhere we went. And me, custard
    cups.
They cost pennies in those days, with the *fascistas* still in
    power,
at least for a few more months. They were watching us, that
    crew. Not sure why.
We'd run into Saramago at the *pastelaria* all the time,
    remember?
He lived nearby. He wasn't famous yet, just finishing up the
    Blimunda novel,
the one with Scarlatti. He'd buy us both a *galão* now and
    then, sweet man.
I can't imagine he had much more than we did.

Nor were we; famous, that is. Not quite yet. It wasn't until
    the band let me sing.
No one was much into drum machines then,
at least not how we went about it, and that big bass
    synthesizer sound,
the two of us tap-tapping on part-filled milk bottles in time to
    the chorus.
I forget who it was dreamt that one up,
clink-clink, *clink-clink*, each bottle a different level of water,
    different pitch.
But it worked. Blow me, it worked . . .
What were we, 22, 23?

We walked all the way down from the summer palace.
Dark green avenues, fern colonnades, those ponds with water
    lilies . . .

Lord Georgie-Porgie wasn't half-wrong. It was like Eden, but
    even Eden can get old.
We were starving when we found that hole-in-the-wall just off
    the square,
and the bossy little owner with his charcoal brazier.
He nearly dragged us in there and made us sit still for what
    seemed like an hour,
grilling those chunks of cuttlefish, basting and basting them
    in their own ink.
You squealed like a little pig later on when you got a good
    look at your tongue.
—*I'm gonna die, I'm gonna die!*

It rained most every day that January, just like it's raining
    now,
The Terreiro do Paço nearly underwater.
I'd never been anywhere like this before. I don't know that
    I'd really been anywhere.
Climbing up all those slippery cobbled steps every night to
    that pensão the nuns ran,
half-pissed, the white peacocks shrieking in the castle garden
and the sound they made in the rain. It moves me still, this
    place,
the jumble of pastel doorways with their sagging jambs and
    worn stone sills.
The people too, so modest and obliging, a bit melancholy—
no, not so much melancholy, subdued, perhaps, a lid on top.
They do fancy their hats, all right, the old gents.

We clung together like children then.

And you could be so awful, especially if your dick wasn't in
me or you weren't drinking.

I'd cry and cry, not because of how you were or what you said.

I felt like I was always melting inside.

Yeah, yeah, sure—*But oft, in lonely rooms, and 'mid the din /
of towns and cities . . .*

My apologies, Mr. Chalmers, you did your best . . .

You know how water finds its way through a seam in the roof.

I mean, do I really want to split open again like a sodden
aubergine?

Does anyone need to see that again?

These drives to the airport are all the same, no matter what
town you're in.

*—Luis, darling, can you turn up the sound a bit? You know
who that is, don't you?*

Of course, luv, of course you do.

MICINO

I found under the tongue, when he opened wide,
a harvest of minuscule Thai red peppers
clustered either side of his pink frenulum,
twin fields of fiery stalagmites.
And as if that were not passing strange enough,
behind and above two shelves of tiny Lucite drawers
to my alarm one of which you chose to open
and examine closely in its moist mucosa casing
before gently replacing it, and without consequence
as to structure or disquiet on *sleeping* Micino's part,
I suppose given our past history of how routinely
I would pry open his jaws to massage his gums,
then run my finger along his sharp, serried molars,
those twelve incisors, rub up and down both fangs
between forefinger and thumb, then for luck tap
the tips of both as I made to take leave of that warm portal
and carry my attentions elsewhere, first stroking his flanks,
then, discreetly, his belly, and tickling behind both his ears.

Micino, Micino, so bounteous the love that flowed between us,
and a trust I would in the end betray so cruelly . . .
But here he was again, spread lengthwise across the floor
at the foot of the backseat in our powder-blue Chevy wagon
looking scrawny, gray, dusty, more mummified than living;
that is, until he blinked. BLINKED. Micino risen . . .
At which point I raised him to my lap:

—Micino, Micino, you're alive, I cried,
and then he lifted his eyes in the direction of mine, ever so
    weakly,
it seemed as if life itself was barely flickering inside him.
But as I began to stroke him he seemed to suddenly revive.
—Where have you been, my darling boy, Micino?
For had I not left him long ago on the Bardo Plane,
his mortal flesh dissolving at the foot of the fan palm
in the shallow grave I dug for him there, the rhizomes
of the bamboos close by slowly, slowly pulling apart his bones?
—Holland, I think, he offered wearily and with no certainty
as we unhurriedly made our way along the banks of the *lordly*
    Hudson.

LA BELLE VILLE

Passenger jets float silently across the thunderheads
in the direction of Chibougamau and Matagami Lake,
one after another. Who can say why:
the Midsummer Meti Mosquito Festival, featuring
live performances and dance workshops, handicrafts . . .
I watch them pass overhead through the skylight
as I stretch out on the yoga mat, aligning my sore bones.
The loud snap of a wheel clamp on the street below
drives the Rottweiler next door into a paroxysm of rage.
The sun now above the tree line, the world again renews,
bicycling from point A to point B, a box lunch of Brie and
ham on a kaiser roll, twelve grapes, a Fanta, attached to the
    rear rack.
It continues on like this until the leaves begin to fall
and the first snow arrives, but much the same, different
    footwear.
Off they go to the groovy software design studio and
    columbarium,
enorbed by their things-to-do lists and amorous set-backs.
It's all enough to drive one to a dusty cubicle, chanting
    Sutras . . .
Oh, but oh, the cycle of Samsara, with its lesions,
    exhortations,
lost appointment books, gratuitous slights, bouts of catalepsy,
her goodie-tray wrapped in a variety of silks or light cottons.

I am the Body of the World, pinioned like poor Gulliver in
    Lilliput.
Semi-trailers and tank cars filled with ethanol course
    through me.
I cannot move. A plaque from their exhaust accumulates in
    my arteries,
the particulate matter taking on the viscosity of despair.

CHAPTER 53

[Stamboul]

They *are* unattractive,
these prosperous couples spread about at breakfast,
familiar to one another as old bathrobes,
color faded, nap nearly gone. It does no harm to say so.

And lordly, pecking and scrolling away between bites,
calling in dispatches from their frontier outposts,
each a caliphate unto himself.
All appears to be in order, as God would will it.

Their *pashas* know better than to disturb them,
not here, not now, not in this distant refuge at their leisure,
this privileged eyrie looking south
at domes and minarets, the harbor below,

history funneling through its narrow strait,
where *Europe kisses Asia*,
war fleets, like swarms of bees, hovering beyond the walls,
awaiting the signal . . .

The server is experiencing technical problems.
Please try again in a few moments.

Thanks for your continued patience.
We're sorry for any inconvenience this may cause.

Galleys bob out on the Marmora, oars dipped,
dragon-headed prows making ready to spit fire.
Siege engines take up position outside the Gate of St. Romanus.
Sappers burrow below.

There is now much disquiet in the room.
Young women servants hurry about, squeaking apologies.
This seems to be a characteristic of the young women here,
this squeaking. They are no doubt trained to do so.

Ibrahim, addicted to lust as Murat was to wine,
espied the privy parts of a certain wild heifer
and so inflamed he thus became
urgently sent forth the shape of them pressed into gold

across his vast kingdom with order to take inventory
until such a one was found, an Armenian,
it turned out, from the village of Arnavutköy,
a 333 lb. oven of enchantment.

He very nearly lost his wits until Mother stepped in
and had the poor thing throttled over dinner.
Surely, the servers will return to use presently.
This is not a Third World country

and we are paying through the nose to be here.
It seems the Genoese cannot be trusted.
A great plank greased with animal fat has been laid secretly
over the shoulder of the hill behind us, only a few blocks off.

The enemy's ships have been dragged down it in the night,
portaged to the inlet below.
Sultan es Selatin, king of kings, sovereign of sovereigns,
most high emperor of Byzantium and Trebizond,

very powerful king of Persia, of Arabia, of Syria, and of
    Egypt,
supreme lord of Europe, and of Asia,
prince of Mecca and Aleppo, lord of Jerusalem,
ruler of the universal sea,

sits atop a pile of carpets, stacked high
in front of the carpet shop, whiskers bristling, and, taking in
the fearful events around him, eyes narrowing to slits,
blinks.

SERGIO LEONE

—*Lamb Posse is what tops the bill this a.m., Sheriff,*
plus your shot of choice, plus a slice of pie, pecan or rhubarb,
    you pick.
—*I'll skip the pie, thank ye, and have a beer back instead o'.*
—*Don't know that I can swing that, bud.*
—*Swing it, brother, swing, you dozy cull,*
slapping down my sidearm on the counter, loudie-like, to make
    a point.
A head or two beginning to turn my way
but one gander at that big silver gun barrel, swiveled right back.
There was a hunnert mile of high dry plain on every side of us
    out there,
heat slithering up your back, then garroting you about noon,
like faux wild west España: rattlesnake maracas, bad teeth,
squirrelly red-eyed night varmints, ruined old battlements
ever so often, a day or so's journey on horseback between,
'stead of our own gas station/convenience store lash-ups . . .
talking days of yore España, storybook fare, swords, infidels,
    history . . .
but we don't do history, never have done, none to be had or
    made use of.
What we do got is now, right here, pucker up that brain and
    have a lookie-see:
horizon to horizon, *nada* amigo, before or after, just the law,
    and the law is me.

SNOW APPROACHING

ON THE HUDSON

Passenger ferries emerge from the mist
  river and sky, seamless, as one—
    watered ink on silk

then disappear again, crossing back over
  to the other shore, the World of Forms—
    as-if-there-were, as-if-there-were-not

The buildings on the far shore ghostly
  afloat, cinched by cloud about their waists—
    rendered in the *boneless* manner

Cloud need not resemble water
  water need not resemble cloud—
    breath on glass

The giant HD plasma screen atop Chelsea Piers
  flashing red and green—
    stamped seal in a Sesshu broken ink scroll

A tug pushes the garbage scow, left to right, toward the sea
  passing in and out of the Void—
    vaporizing gray, temporal to timeless

Clouds wait, brooding for snow
  and hang heavily over the earth—
    Ch'ien Wei-Yen

Bustle of traffic in the sky, here, as well, on the shore below
  obliterated—
    empty silk

The wind invisible
  spume blown horizontal in the ferry's wake—
    wind atmosphere, river silk

FATHER

He handed me his stick,
the street worker in the hour before dawn,
the stick with which he picked trash from the gutter
to put into his bag, the tool by which he earned his way.
My friend H was much intrigued.
—*Are you going to give it back to him?*
—*No*, I said, and continued on.
H caught up behind me, voicing his concern,
a foreign town, the consequences unforeseeable.
What, for instance, if he came back after us
and brought his friends?
                              —*Thief!* he would remonstrate.
What sort of man would take a humble worker's stick,
and force his children to go without?

We hurried our pace.
True enough, he did come back after us, and not alone.
We fled over tar-papered roof decks and parapets,
down alleys, through private gardens, trampling flower beds,
dogs barking and H none too pleased,
gasping for breath, muttering imprecations as we went.

Soon enough we had shaken our pursuers, and then H too
    vanished.
And then, after some wandering, I came upon familiar terrain,
places I routinely happen upon in the course of these night
    journeys:

the circusy corner dive bar, one part Latin Quarter, three
    parts Brecht;
a verdant passage winding steeply uphill, not far from the
    Observatory;
a perch on the city's crest, looking south toward the radio
    tower;
the lacerating disclosure and acid bath of sexual jealousy . . .
I know well the sites and circumstances;
still, the sequencing and iterations confound me.

And then, as is nearly always the case, I find myself home,
home being the old family house, and with no one around.
I had not phoned to say I would be gone
and am pained by my own thoughtlessness.
I know I shall be chastised on account of it
when Mother and Father do, finally, return,
which presently they do,
the car crunching gravel in the driveway.
But as they walk into the kitchen
they barely take account of me, so busy are they squabbling:
nothing serious, mind you, but each anxious to have his say.

Father, we get along so well these days,
the two of us very nearly the same age,
a powerful, more nearly fraternal kind of love between us now
and you ever so much more sympathetic.
I keep meaning to ask you
and always somehow manage to forget: what sort of dreams
    were you dreaming

when, as a small child, I climbed weekend mornings into your
    bed?
Were they anything like my own, the kind that visit me of late?
And did you yourself remain a child in them,
casting foolishly, randomly about as I do, helpless and
    untethered,
even as an old man, even toward the end?

Sesquipedalian Thomas, aureate Urquhart,
Sir Thomas of Cromarty,

author of *THE TRISSOTETRAS:*
  OR
A MOST EXQUISITE TABLE FOR
RESOLVING ALL MANNER OF TRIANGLES,
and the most commendable
LOGOPANDECTEISION
OR AN INTRODUCTION TO THE UNIVERSAL LANGUAGE,
dedicated to *Nobody*,

and, not least, his *PANTOCHRONACHANON:*
or, A PECULIAR PROMPTUARY OF TIME
which, with rare exactitude, traces the *URQUHART* line
from *the Creation of the World* and Adam,
"*surnamed the* Protoplast" unto 1652:
these including Esormon, Prince of Achaia (2139 B.C.)
and Pamprosodos Urquhart, who married Termuth,
the Pharaoh's daughter who found Moses among the bulrushes.

Royalist, bane of the Covenanters, stalwart,
Christianus Presbyteromstix:
the "Raid of Turiff," Inverness, Aberdeen,
veteran of the battle of Worcester;

thrice imprisoned in the Tower of London;
who would perish from laughter
upon being told of the restoration of the King;
found him a puddle outside the Cat & Mustard Pot,
sat
and waged pitiful tyranny against the phlegm, vibrato, and tears
that bespoke drink on a heavy heart.

Chivvied by creditors, pilloried by malison of every kind,
his noddle much modified by the liquor of grape,
he gan to unleash his word-hoard
and visit upon the worst his fullest measure of clapperclaw;

then, drawing both his oak-handled dirk and *sgian dhu*
from his gargantuan purse of Rhetorick,
fell about them with trope and paramologetick,
diminishing them tapinotically and by paraphrasis,
next by means of similie and cromatick,

followed hard by sulfurous hail of scorn:
slabberdegullion druggels, freckled bittors, drawlatch hoydons,
ninny lobcocks, scurvy sneaksbies, blockish grutnols, doddipol
joltheads, slutch calf-lollies, grouthead gnat-snappers, noddie-
peak simpletons, turdy-gut shitten shepherds;

and still worse, threatening
to plunge his *Roger* into their *packet-rackets* one by one
until they set off a great *pioling* in the manner of pelicans.

And having routed them thus,
good Sir Thomas shook himself with a meaty hiccup
straight in the air, up nearly a foot,
then dropped him smartly on the coccyx.

—*This knight is poorly*, Tom said,

and let go his precious Scot cookies
near to whole
like a molten archipelago on rainy cobbles.

"EAST WIND OVER WEEHAWKEN"

A quandary, to be sure: kissing,
tenderly, hungrily atop the bluff on a greensward off Boulevard
    East,
right by the steps of the old Grauert Causeway, winding down
to the waterfront far below, the Hopper painting, two streets
    south
on 49th. He must have climbed up all those steps, sketchbook in
    hand.
She was luscious, my word, was she ever, dark as a Moor and
    filled with ardor—
for me, if you can imagine. Who can say why? We had only just
    met,
in the corner of a nearby bar and were almost immediately hard
    at it.
Barely a word had passed between us. I suppose these things
    happen,
but not to me or, I daresay, you. The others at the bar were
    most bemused.
The problem lay just up the road a few bus stops: a wife and
    child,
dinner nearly ready. I loved them dearly and I believe that night
    was veal,
shank or saltimbocca, I can no longer recall. And new potatoes.
I loved my wife. I loved my boy. And they loved me, utterly.
    What to do?

Her eyes are lovely, dark and deep. I yearned to be lost in
    those woods again
and come upon a sunlit meadow, my head swimming in aromas,
floral and musk. I know this terrain, too well. If a phantasm,
    just go. I'm old.

QUASI AFFLATZI

White smoke billowed from the chophouse chimney,
bringing with it the scent of hickory and charred roast.
It was done, then; and the choice congenial
to my own, firming, views on secondary school curricula.
I knew the man, of course, not well, but clearly not a criminal
or psychopath like any number of others.
I foresaw many evenings, the two of us,
seated in a quiet booth, in the selfsame chophouse, opposite
one another on red banquettes, dark mahogany motif,
the waitress wearing next to nothing but a shy smile,
tinsel woven haphazardly through her pale brown pubes.
—*Another double Maker's for you, Friar Tuck?* she would ask.
—*And for you, Chief, another birch beer?*

Which, a fortnight later, is exactly how it played out:
same booth, same waitress, fresh tinsel . . .
—*Tino Michelino* (né Michele Ambrosiano, Padua, 1944),
the fuchsia piping and gray ponytail, white and blue
    yachtsman's cap.
The newly chosen Cisalpine Minister of the Public Good
    seemed touched
I called him as he was called on the footie field back when.
(We remain, finally, all of us, who once we were on the footie
    pitch,
whether we wield scepter or scythe, and lonely is he who wields
    the former.)

—*Shoot*, says he.

        I'm talking full-on Ascham, says me:
Archery, Aesop, Cicero, Titus Livius, Melanchthon's
   Commonplaces,
the grooming of leaders through a grounding in classics,
then add a soupçon of Mulcaster, you know: 'To daunce
   comlie: to sing,
and play of instrumentes cunnyingly.'

        —*You kill me, Tuck,*
   you do, you really truly do,
says he.

AFTER RÉAUMUR

They are, perforce, panicked by my interventions,
as well they might be.
I have studied their formations for quite some time now,
watched how they gather for assault
in teeming clumps and chains, broken ovals,
narrow columns straight as a stick.
I have observed them as they issue from the bivouacs and
    earthen galleries
to lay waste an enemy or replenish their stores.

It was in Abyssinia
with their tireless forays and terrible slaughter
I first took their measure and scrutinized their ways;
how they pinched or sheared the heads off their victims
then dragged them back to their underground chambers,
of which there are thousands,
to feed their young and hosts of slaves.

In combat I have observed them extrude the fangs
of their mandibles, flex their abdomens
until the cuticle girdling them burst, choking their prey
in a corrosive, foaming lather;
or, likewise, from the nozzle
of their cherished anal vesicle spew
divers poison filaments—
endocrine tankers on locust legs;

or force from its sheath, like a canine's pizzle,
the stinger that sits above their gaster,
convulsing their victim forthwith.

The dreadful pismire,
some the size of wolfhounds,
some no bigger than a grain of sand,
with spiked carapaces,
very black, bluish black, red, amber, or chestnut brown,
who know no day of repose,

who gather resin from the pine forests
to strengthen and ornament their terraces,
only to have these nuggets pilfered by the locals
and then sold as incense, called *Thuringian* incense;

this implacable foe of both dormice and cicadas,
the latter whose chattering drives them to a frenzy;

who are suited for nothing apart from war, and perfectly
    suited;
ABDUCT   PUNCTURE   ENSLAVE
but who will then tenderly stroke the backs of aphids
to milk from them a single honeydew droplet;

who will set forth over large distances as solitary scouts
or in numbers that compare only with those clouds of mayflies
which congregate certain spring evenings on the banks of our
    rivers;

of whom the Indians of Malabar are said to partake,
having first cooked then seasoned them with pepper;

who continually exhale a volatile spirit,
a vile, displeasing musk
so penetrating and obnoxious it at once provokes sneezing,
but which is to them as the *high* aroma of cooked partridge is
    to us.

Thus, it was the dogs caught wind of them first,
here where we've set up camp by the estuary;
and here, from amidst the heavy morning ground fog,
they first emerged, as if from the very mud below,
to press their attack
but in the guise of horses, pack mules, livestock,
and in greatest numbers having taken on the aspect of human
    beings,
soldiers like us, and wrapped in our selfsame uniforms,
ammunition belts, even our regiment's insignia,
antennae folded like carpenter rules under their helmets,
scalpel-sharp mandibles hidden down the sleeves of their
    greatcoats.

The hour of slaughter is at hand, ours or theirs.
The traps set.
The trenches of poison, sweetly beckoning,
irresistible as the song of the Sirens,
milky with borax, flowing with the oils of clove and
    peppermint,

an enchanting quicksand of bifenthrin . . .
Press forward my darlings and drink, drink your fill,
first one and then the whole of them, as they will,
for this is their nature, their greatest strength and gravest flaw,
servants of the One Single Mind,
bearers of the common Mother Scent, estranging them from all
    others . . .

And just as they are drawn to the earliest shoots of an apricot
    tree
whose pistils they tear asunder so that they may drink the sap,
so do these Lacedaemonians now draw close
and assemble before us, verily a cloud of death
casting its shadow across our encampment—
First a thalassic rustling sound, then their suffocating vapor . . .
I bring you warm greetings from Field Marshal Zhukov.
Make ready to boil in our rivers of nectar.

MEET THE JONESES

Acetaminophen Jones

Kohlrabi Jones

Cuneiform Jones

No-See-Em Jones

Psilocybin Jones

Too Tall Jones

Zanzibar Jones

Bösendorfer Jones

Fizzy Paris Jones

Tegucigalpa Jones

Farfallina Jones

Jugurtha Jones

Chimichurri Jones

Malatesta Jones

Prestodigitalis Jones

Hammurabi Jones

Muffaletta Jones

Anaxagoras Jones

Rapunzella Jones

Volatile Jones

Chalumeaux Jones

'Styrene Jones

No-Show Jones

Nikitaconazole Jones

Simplex Jones

Razzparilla Jones

Chin-Chiller Jones

Def Jones

Calamitous Jones

Stegosaurus Jones

Neutrino Jones

Trismegistus Jones

Kronik Jones

Zoophagous Jones

Scrofulus Jones

Supernal Jones

LAUNDERETTE

The two loads of washing I had in haste left behind
were to be found on a shelf at the back of the launderette
neatly folded into four large grocery bags,
the more thickly cottoned polo shirts still somewhat damp,
what I gladly at first took as a random kindness quickly clouded
    over
with what can only have been necessity and the terrible
    inconvenience
I had brought to bear through my negligence, my persistent
    awful, awful . . .
On an already overburdened and deeply melancholic attendant
who would not have anticipated for herself this life of chores
in an over-bright, noisy arena of perfumed foam and the thud
    of driers,
small children out of hand, shopping guides and animal waste,
and on the TV overhead the number one ladies' morning chat
    show
featuring the twin goddesses of our exhausted imagination,
Kathie Lee and Whoopi, hosting celebrity authors, recovering
    selfie addicts,
their frantic quipping reaching a climax just in time for
    commercial break . . .
—*Herr Klein-y, might I interject here for a moment?*
I remember now where this was, it was the town famous for its
    Methodists,

unhoused lunatics and transsexuals, a halfway decent lunch
   counter
around the block and unobstructed ocean views: "God's
   Square Mile"
it read on a large wooden placard as one drove into town.
—*You do get around, don't you?* the doctor said to me (did
   I sense opprobrium?)
the right side of his jaw gone missing, shot off in war or a
   hunting misadventure
or perhaps eroded by the force of endless chatter and
   misinformation,
though it did lend to his countenance an off-center, equine,
   even rakish look,
when I was reminded just then, perhaps by the art, perhaps
   the science
of this legendary maestro, the most gifted disciple of you-
   know-who in Berne,
how weary I had become, not so much of the staircases and
   grand hotels,
but my failures at navigation and proper scheduling, both.

AGAINST SOCIALIZATION

Your alarming non sequitur sits there, defiant,
not unlike a tiny incandescent meteorite,
trembling with radioactive menace on the end table.
Do not be alarmed; rather give yourself over to gratitude.
Regard this as a kind of gift, from the very heavens above.
That dismay on the faces of those others in the room around
    you
will abate, and, over time, transform into something like
    wonder.

Like a date gone horribly wrong, where your every word and
    gesture
refracts into what seems an inadvertent, ghastly insult
until she pulls her chair back from the table and stands there,
too stunned by the affront to register the rage and disgust
that later take on clarity and burn like a sharp slap to the
    cheek.
This episode will resuscitate itself for several decades at least,
first as a darkly instructive moment under the heading:

Appalling and gratuitous male behavior, Exhibit A,
or as a *can-you-top-this* war story over brunch.
And yes, they will all shake their heads in dismay and
    disbelief,
perhaps even a bleak chuckle or two: *Krikee, what pigs* . . .

But that too will transfigure over time into a more
    significant event,
one that not so much informed her sense
    of—what?—outrage? No,
no, as with the other, a marvel, a windfall, an undreamt-of
    visitation.

CLUB MESSINA

—What city is this? I inquired.
I might better have asked what country . . .
She either didn't hear or chose not to heed.
I could tell by the light just over the rise
we were close, a block or two from water,
a river or harbor, a few old battlements
commanding two separate heights nearby.
I had forgotten to change my dollars to the local currency,
a failure of mine so obstinately, repeatedly insistent,
even in the face of . . .
The Versateller was guarded by three women,
each with a pistol, bandolier, and evil look about her.
I ignored them as is my custom and began to punch
my code into the keypad, but there was no number 5.
—What happened to the 5? I inquired. No reply.
The women in this town seemed notably unresponsive.
Of course, there was that book I dearly wanted to get hold of,
the famously illustrated one about medieval siege engines,
and a bookstore, swank, mahogany-paneled walls,
attached to the Hotel Central, open still at this eldritch hour,
but not a clerk in sight, and, if I might be allowed,
so poorly stocked that one could easily infer
the very act of reading here had drifted into desuetude.

MURPH & ME

Windshield wipers slapping back and forth, Murph's Celebrity
   Sedan
hugged the curve as it sped onto the Edison Bridge, Super 88
   4 barrel
High Compression 394 Rocket V8, Roto Hydro-Matic
   transmission, power steering,
Pedal-Ease power brakes, the rolling black cylinder
   speedometer
flashing green, yellow, and red, holding steady at 65 mph,
   midnight-blue frame
encasing me in terror, where I remain still, sleeping or awake
when I conjure that ride across the old deck plate and girder
   bridge
with its big hump in the middle, all 29 spans, the muddy
   Raritan 135 feet below,
Murph's foot to the floor as he wove through the pack,
   growling
imprecations, outraged by the pace of the rest of the world,
   frantic
to get nowhere in particular except in the early a.m. on the
   GW Bridge
dropping me off at the IRT on 168th then heading downtown to
   his taxi place.
He was at his best, or worst ("wurst," he would have said), in
   that meat-grinder,
a heavy-lidded Steve McQueen gone to seed, bald, paunch,
   sporty double-knit

casual wear of an indeterminate era, banging on his Roto-
Matic steering wheel.

—*So who's that little broad with freckles and orange hair?*

(Lord God-Lady, forgive me, forgive Murph: Flatbush Ave.,
Brooklyn,

born the same day as that misfortune with the Archduke,
right?)

—*Maxine*, I say.—*Are you doing her?*—*Christ, Murph, I'm
only 14!*

This plainly displeased him. You could say Murph was my
unofficial guardian,

the Jack Teagarden to my Stan Getz, sans horns, a somewhat
unsavory coupling,

and one not without implications down the road . . .

But you can imagine how purgatorial, that rolling, rackety,
fitful journey uptown

after the 25 minutes pinned back in the death seat beside
Murph,

taking in the world, at speed, the river beneath, always
trying to beat his record,

with me beside him in that selfsame seat, the blur of tail fins,
cables, sky

through that curvilinear windshield, across bridges for the
most part, but not just.

Every year Murph would flip cars, trading in the 88 for a 98
Custom Sports Coupe,

345 horsepower Starfire engine, dual rear cigarette lighters,
leather interior.

Malcolm X drove the very same car, before things went south
with Elijah M.

Hard to imagine Murph and Malcolm would have much to say
to one another.

No matter where we were—Anchorage, the Azores—Murph
had the radio on.

Sports mostly, we'd talk sports, but the news too. Murph
hated Robert Kennedy.

Murph said he'd win because he made "all the broads cream
in their jeans."

Dad hated Kennedy too, all of 'em, Poppa Joe to his toothy,
roguering whelps.

But Dad loved Murph, and Murph loved Dad. That's why he
let Murph drive me.

One day Murph brought Dad back a baby alligator from
Miami.

—*Whadayawant from Florida, Marv?* Murph asked.—*An
alligator*, Dad said.

Mother wasn't happy. She put the little reptile behind the
fridge hydrator

and fed it bits of raw hamburger until one day it escaped and
bit the dog's nose,

bit it bad so it never looked quite right again. That was that
for the alligator.

But Murph, he seemed to like the General Casimir Pulaski
Skyway best,

a steel truss cantilever affair, a monstrous Erector set from
Hell,

the Meadowlands and railyards below, Hoffa's bones likely
somewhere near.

Any excuse. He'd blast past the Budweiser sign and drop me
at the heliport,

then head down to Bayonne for a round of pinochle with his
old rag-trade pals
in a cloud of cigar smoke, going through the booty "what fell
off a truck."
—*I got a Sylvania 9000 F.M., Marv, fell off a truck, $22,
can't beat the price.*
He'd try to best 28 minutes crossing the Pulaski, the GW
record was 12 and some,
no small feat along that bottle-necked death trap. Oh, I ride
with Murph still,
across the Verrazzano to the family grave plots, the Brooklyn
Bridge, where once,
half-way across, he asks, out of the blue,—*Howz the poetry
game treating you?*
Then, in that old-timey, low-rent Flatbush accent, starts
declaiming:
*Through the bound cable strands, the arching path /
Upward, veering with light . . .*
I'm talking the first three stanzas . . . *The loft of vision,
palladium helm of stars.*
I could never figure out how he pulled that one out of the air,
to this very day.
The Lions Gate, the Seven Mile Bridge across the Keys, and
even farther afield:
Crossing Lake Maracaibo on the General Rafael Urdaneta,
the Akashi-Kaikyo . . .
He's still there beside me, roaring across the Lupu,
Bloukrans, Øresund:
—*Check out the knockers on that broad; it's a wonder she
don't tilt right over.*

BOY

I lent him some bone from my one good leg
as a shillelagh or battering ram, just in case,
which seemed to calm him down.
That first day is never a picnic, this we know.

Why, wasn't it only last fall . . .
Now, his own legs seem to no longer belong,
certainly not to him, as if abandoning
his torso, gone off to wander on their own.

He stands before me, festooned
with pneumatocysts, red, testosterone, blue, cortisol,
pompadour and cowlick rigid with gel,
orange knee socks, "laser green" running shoes.

I do love him—would that I didn't—
but not when he lifts me over his head
and makes like to throw me against the wall.
Mother says: —*Goddamn it, JackJack, what the hell!*

He grows and grows. Soon he will simply step over me
as if I were an ottoman or dozing pet.
Is that not a look of scorn I see?
Off into the world, thermos filled with meatballs, he goes.

HEAT

The blue-bellied fence lizards have died back
into stone or the walls they attach themselves to,
drinking in mineral and sun, proliferating
almost before one's eyes,
a slow-motion saurian mitosis
a reticulated vine with eyes and split tongues,
threatening to blanket every surface.

Gone, overnight it would seem,
like the sun at day's end below the horizon
but not returning: a conjury, the Lord
retracting his edict of *fiery serpents* upon the Israelites—
disappeared into a compost of shadow.

The summer's heat retreats slowly here in the valley,
a dusting of snow already on the mountain summits.
Tirelessly, the roots of camphor and live oak
probe in the loam for moisture—
roof tiles, brass doorknobs, hot as griddles,
silence in the village.

SHADOW MAN

Shadow man's still there,
his back to it all, huddled over the picnic table,
even after Halloween, after the first big December rain,
the pre-Christmas all day Church & Baseball Posada,
mariachi trumpet, impassioned orators:
GOD LOVES BASEBALL. GOD LOVES YOU.

Still there, under the sycamores,
big dun leaves plastering the basketball court,
staring, as he does, at nothing.

I envy him that nothing,
and the way his days take shape around it.
In the heat of midsummer,
awakening on his bench courtside,
moving across the way to the shade of a live oak
as the sun lifts overhead.

Not always easy to spot him there in the shadows,
at least not straightaway:
black tracksuit, black skin, black do-rag
he goes off to soak in the fountain every so often,
the day stretching before him,
sun making its transit across the sky.

One might well think him mad, living the way he does,
soundless,
marooned somewhere inside his head,
up to nothing, nothing in hand,
moving spot to spot over the course of the day,
his stations in the park,
finding the sun when it's chill, the shade when hot,
nothing more,
very nearly a mendicant of nothing.

I think not;
mad, that is, at least not when his eyes have met mine
those mornings I've been out there,
just the two of us at that early hour.
A man is there, present in that gaze,
careworn, to be sure, but in no way raddled or elsewhere.
Nor is he displeased to see me here,
come to pay a visit to the place he lives,
come with my ball to shoot awhile and watch the leaves
drift down, amber, dun, and gold, the sun
sometimes catching a train of motes in their wake,
the sough of traffic along Claremont Boulevard.

I'll wave. He may or may not wave back.
Usually not, or maybe offer the barest of nods.
Some days more than others weigh heavily upon him,
I can tell that by now.
One day I thought I even overheard a sob,
which is all the noise I've ever heard come out of him.

Shadow Man is out there now, always out there.
I can tell you where by the hour on the clock,
under which tree, what corner of the park,
almost as if he's waiting for someone,
someone who, when ready, will know to come find him there.

The semester is winding down.
Mid-afternoon sun already low in the sky.
A week since the clatter of cleats at dusk.
The train rattles along behind First Street sounding its horn,
to L.A. or east to San Bernardino.
The top of Mt. Baldy hidden behind cloud.

TODAY'S LUNCH SPECIAL
Polenta-Stuffed Tomato & Pulled Pork

Students clustered at tables, TV overhead.
Chlamydia in bloom throughout the dining hall.
Professor Murchison, Emeritus,
far too old and too tall to be doing this,
and at such a late hour,
not long before closing,
bent over a text in the library stacks,
turning the pages slowly
but with some urgency.
                    —*I just needed to tell you,*
Buffy, the women's soccer coach,
says to her striker,
a lanky brunette who calls herself Suze,
how much . . .

Coach pauses, caught up, it would seem,
by emotion, perhaps fear.
The tiny angel on her right shoulder
in an oversized football jersey,
school colors, navy blue and emerald green:
—*Not again, Buff,*
You know what happened the last time.
And the tiny devil on her left,
orange leotards, black angora sweater vest:
—*Well?*

It was just a block or two off Palisade Ave.,
a sprawling, second-floor living room,
faux wood-paneled, stuffed chairs, big sofa,
cheap ceramic Disney figurines on the coffee table,
but with a wall-sized picture window facing east,
the midtown "moody, water-loving giants of Manhattan"
nearly in our laps, a 3-D mirage, a Fata Morgana
of the sort you see sometimes on Rte. 46 headed south for the
    GW Bridge,
ghostly buildings in the sky ahead of you the size of Himalayas.

The principal actors were locals, acquaintances, once featured in
Kraft Foods Midday Matinee, stretching torturously toward
    some bleak horizon,
reminiscent of those stupefying 12-hour art films of the '70s
time-lapse photography of a ladybug over many months,
first venturing left a millimeter, then right,
then collapsing of her own weight and disintegrating
atop the flaccid member of a junked-out blond love object.

All of us much alike, in manner, background, dress,
sans ambition, personality—well, perhaps a dismal aggregate
    of TV knock-offs,
supporting-role types: *Fatty, Perky, Poufy, Pesty* . . .
having lived lives, if not wasted, distinguished in no way
    whatsoever:

"Middle-Aged Sears Shoppers in Repose Among
     Themselves,"
an installation piece best kept in the garage, ersatz
     Kienholz,
or "Portrait of a New Jersey Interior, Cliffside Park, 1974"
     by Chauncey Hare.

Ordinariness seemed to cling to us like dinge or some kind
     of mold,
I no more nor less than the others.
But I am now compelled here to confess: what altered me,
rendered me a sort of dybbuk or freak, this capacity I had
     for—
what?: time travel, astral projection, roaming
     impostiture—*knock, knock/*
who's there?—ever in disguise, as if dispatched by some
     o'er-governing impulse,
that radiated and infused my inner being, veiled but
     present,
decals of exotic ports of call sprouting across the inside of
     my skull—

not unlike the old, cordovan-colored suitcase belonging to
     my late Great-Uncle Nandor—
along with the attendant, requisite tricks of mimicry,
     vanishing
in a trice, transformation, all picked up on the fly, beyond
     any *normal*'s ken

and, of course, hidden *in a vest pocket*, as it were, that served
   to make me master
of the room in which we all together sat that very same
   afternoon, the house
in which it belonged, and any number of other rooms and
   houses just like them . . .

It was a fortnight before *le couple coiffure* turned up for the
   high season.
A small flat her tante in Paris owned and let to the couple
   every year,
and for many years. They were not young. Mlle.'s
   discomfort was evident
from the moment they stepped off the bus that night, as if
   she found him
unworthy somehow of such a gift as a free flat in St. Tropez,
   or her, or both,
or perhaps a general peevishness had seeped in during the
   long journey down.
Famous now, a matron, whose name conjures hopes or
   fears, buoys
or stifles careers, but then not much more than a child, one
   who already knew
large success awaited, or what she counted success, and had
   abandoned him,
not recently, if it had ever really taken notice. Still, she
   loved him,
in her own fashion, if often querulously or diluted by
   suspicion.
But her French was perfection, thus bestowing on him a
   kind of invisibility,

his preferred mode. It would remain so and over time only
   intensify
until he came to resemble a decommissioned spy or some
   Burroughs character,
one of his old gray junkies in rumpled gabardine and
   wearing a fedora.
There was little to occupy the two of them, really: read,
   stroll, make love,
shop at the little open market below their balcony in the old
   quarter
where a tolerable bleu Auvergne could be found dirt-cheap
   and made
for a lovely sauce or dressing. Their Baedeker was that
   torrid Salter novel
with Philip and Anne-Marie whipping up a froth in
   Burgundy's grand old hotels,
roaring down two-lane country roads in a vintage Delage,
   top down,
café to café, bar to bar, meal to meal, bed to bed, hurtling
   aimlessly
through a spring and summer at speed under canopies of
   plane trees
until . . . well . . . One knew it was destined to end, and
   very badly.
He, for his part, mostly hid in the old
   chapel-turned-museum, L'Annunciade,
beholding what Dufy, especially Dufy, Camoin, Monguin,
   Marquet, and that

crowd, did with the light, just after dawn and at end of day,
    sea light, and had

been, after Signac led the way. —*When I realized each
    morning I would see this*

light again I could not believe my luck, wrote Matisse.
    Though Mlle. couldn't be

bothered, with that light or any particular light to speak of
    or any artist's

rendering.

Am I being unkind? Surely. Please forgive me. Whither
    Colette? With her cats

in that secluded garden, the great lady, no longer young (his
    age) suffering still

through those overmastering bouts of passion . . . —*The
    cats will spring sideways at the moths when by ten the
    air is blue as a morning glory. —After dinner*, Sidonie-

Gabrielle wrote—*I mustn't forget to irrigate the little
    runnels that surround the*

*melons, and to water by hand the balsam, phlox and
    dahlias and the young*

*tangerine trees, which haven't got roots yet long enough to
    drink . . .*

Then we have the youthful Agnelli, only recently back from
    the Front

(Can you imagine: spoiled, pretty Gianni on the Eastern
    Front?), vibrating

like a tuning fork from all the cocaine, while he snorkeled
    his heart away offshore,

sending up a multitude of bubbles between the legs of all
    those Ginas,
Moniques and Yvettes. Of course, these were the early days,
    before the big crash
along the corniche, the long convalescence and then the
    triumphs:
Fiat's *Avvocado*, the "King of Italy," his Patek Phillipe
    worn halfway up his sleeve
and his dick up Jackie O below deck. How she thrived on
    the open sea, that one.
And then, in their wake: hustlers, deadbeats, remittance
    men, *le couple coiffure*,
tyro cineastes, package tours from Sheffield and
    Dusseldorf, 374 bad novelists
and, bringing up the rear, our two curiously feathered
    American lovebirds,
out of tune, out of sorts, out of place, and 50 years late.

DANCE, DANCE, DANCE

The four of us would make that little house shake, dancing
   the night away,
perched there at the foot of the block, right above the cove,
wind blowing at 30 knots, rain peppering the windows like
   BB pellets.
It's a wonder we didn't tip, the house and us with it, onto
   the rocky strand below.
Stax/Volt, King Records' R&B stalwarts: "Finger Poppin'
   Time," "Chain of Fools,"
you taking a solo turn on "Poppa's Got a Brand-New Bag,"
   twitching
to beat the band in your *Isadora-gone-spastic-with rabies*
   mode,
drunkenly crashing into walls, knocking the furniture every
   which way.
I still can't figure out how your wee John slept through it
   all, if he really did.
He somehow made it to Yale, I heard, then studied law. No
   fault of yours . . .
His mother found a proper gent once she managed to
   unload you, that's how.
You dear, impossible, most thoughtless of men. —*What did
   the doctor tell you?*
"He told me I was in perfect health—for a 60-year-old."
   You were then 25.

But somehow lasted another 50, which would have made
    you 110, in dog years,
an image to conjure with, those tight black curls gone white,
    the same mad glare.
If only you'd been with it near the end, able to see on
    television the apotheosis
of your contempt for nearly everything take over center
    stage and set up shop.
You taught me most everything I know about music, at least
    the raw stuff:
The Dixie Hummingbirds, the Louvin Brothers, Ralph
    Stanley singing
"I'm a Man of Constant Sorrow" you claimed made the
    paint peel off your walls.
We'd always finish off the evening with Séamus Ennis of
    County Ennis
skirling his way through "Kiss the Maid Behind the Barrel"
    on his uilleann pipes,
the only sound that could bore its way through that amber
    veil of Bushmills.
You'd have made the best DJ ever to be found in this sad old
    world, ever, ever,
if only you weren't such a hopeless shambles, and a station
    might be found
to accommodate your lurchings: Furtwängler on the heels of
    Guitar Shorty.
I remember one night we all danced so hard the house
    seemed to shift,

if only a bit. It wasn't much of a house, I suppose. Still, the
   landlord wasn't happy.
We danced and danced the nights away on that green, wet,
   sleepy, nowhere isle.
I recall no better or harder dancing, you wobbling, but in
   command, at the helm.

DREAM MACHINE:

EPISODE 22, TAKE #3

I had arrived here as a somewhat aged exchange student,
although I would certainly never have described myself thus,
youthful and curious still as to my appetites,
not to mention expectations, vague as the latter may have been,
if to the locals I may well have seemed otherwise,
a somewhat hobbled, little geezer,
an appearance offset by a brightly colored, not inexpensive
  neck scarf.
I have long and repeatedly been reminded
that my self-image does not square with the actual,
by *actual* one, of course, means in the eyes of obtuse strangers.

But which bus and in which direction?
You see, I no longer had any address in hand.
There most certainly had been one, written down
and, per usual, left under a pile on my night table.
I might have inquired
but the language spoken around me was impenetrable,
chockablock with untamed gutturals and rhotic consonants.

I did make it there in the end. I always do.
Down corridors I recalled from elsewhere,
Wrocław, Passaic, Esquimalt . . .
the graveyard, convenience store, shuttered garage.

Put it down to my capacity for visualization.
I remember in London once, dead drunk,
guiding a minicab driver clueless as a blind cockatoo
from a pub in Hackney all the way to my flop in South Ken.
It involves a kind of trance I get on.

And when I finally arrived at what was to be my residence for
    the term
there to greet me was a roomful of boisterous, clearly
    homosexual men,
mustachioed and in the livery of Prussian cavalry officers,
clinking glasses, much excited by my arrival.
They seemed to know things about me that I barely
    remembered myself.
You might credit it to the modern search engine,
or, if you prefer, something entirely otherworldly.

LOVE CHANT

You can see that big ol' Kwakiutl in the birdsuit
flapping away, swaying right then left
in the bow of a 50-foot war canoe,
his sidekicks banging the handles of their oars in time:
whack   whackwhackwhack   whack whack?

Well, honey, that's about how I feel around you.
Sure, it was all staged, an *ethno-spectacular*
for Curtis and his *actuality* film crew;
blow their minds back in New York along the Great White Way,
King Kong before King Kong.

But that's not how I like to see it,
and I've watched this clip plenty at the museum rainy days like
     this.
How I like to see it, these boys are getting in the mood,
whipping themselves up for a full-on, all-hands, slave raid
     south,
and that would be in our direction.

Look at all those sun-worshippers out there on Ocean Beach,
matrons, truants, ice cream and cotton candy vendors,
doing their thing, checking out the kites and cormorants,
listening to Kruk & Kuip call the game over the radio,
slapping on the cocoa butter.

Out of nowhere they'll come swooping in like pelicans
dive-bombing sardines, gathering up
pink-splotched fatties in Speedos, dogs too,
and tossing them in back of the canoe.
Then, of course, the ceremonial feast:

hormone- and nitrate-free wieners,
little tubs of hummus, rice cakes, PowerBars,
and after that a proper nap, waves gently rocking;
and, first thing on waking, do that dance of theirs they do:
whack   whackwhackwhack   whack whack?

turn that ginormous cedar dugout around
and paddle back the 1000 miles or so to Quatsino Sound,
off-load their haul, hose 'em down,
and get the lot started on polishing the silver, ironing,
picking lice off the kiddies' heads, like that.

As for the more unfortunate adult male slaves, well . . .
Let's just say next harvest moon when the fright masks come
     out
and teeth get to gnashin' & aflashin' in the longhouse,
warriors gathered round the fire crying
     whoop-whoop-dee—whoop . . .
Hey now, my little pullet, *that*, that's how . . .

REVENUE STREAM

He was a not at all unfriendly interlocutor,
aggressive, to be sure, combative even, but an admirer,
clearly, not only of my oeuvre but, curiously, of me,
about whom he could've known next to nothing,
except hearsay and what one might pull off the net,
should one care to pursue such a search. A "stalker," then?
Hardly, but with something about me clearly nagging him,
an itch of sorts that needed to be scratched.

In fact, it became ever clearer over the course of our visit
that instead of a conversation I was being interviewed,
perhaps with a small digital recorder hidden in a pocket
or clipped behind one of the car's overhead sun visors.
We were driving, I should have mentioned, up and down
the West Side Highway, taking this exit or that, doubling back,
aimlessly so far as I could tell, or if by design
certainly none I could determine. But *he* was determined, all
    right,

to find out what, I could not begin to surmise. About how
I went about stringing these words together, as I do,
or some clue to be found in my speech patterns or facial
    gestures?
—*Do you regard yourself as corporate?* he asked.
Like Pfizer or Sun Chemicals of Parsippany, 3.5 billion
    revenue,

board of directors, management team, shareholders?
My drifty, "misguided," *career* counting stresses and syllables?
How bewildering, even provocative, I thought to myself.

Is this ardent, inquisitive young man making sport of me?
Something in his manner and enthusiasm led me to doubt it.
But I did turn the notion over and over again in my mind
as we cruised along in the slow lane: I, the CEO
of a crisply efficient operation, by some manner of alchemy
transmuting my imaginative life into something like a revenue
    stream?
And I did like his car, an '87 Signature Series Lincoln Town
    Car,
6-way power seats and blue carriage roof. It handled like a
    dream . . .

So, there I was—again—right in the middle of Abbott Blvd.
as if I'd just parachuted in from the Carpathian highlands,
and still without my college degree—
the phantom zoo course, the one I bailed on: vestigial gills,
bat sonar, marsupials . . . plaguing me, for what, nearly 50
      years now
(the folks still hadn't caught on to that one, not yet,
but they would, oh, my gracious, would they ever . . .)
on a sodded-over island of trolley track in front of God and
      everyone,
Joe, the old Serb, mowing away in the heat, slugging down
      beers,
Mrs. Sinatra's house directly across the way, panel trucks
      unloading
boxes of Italian cookies, trays of cold cuts, rose and teal
      icing,
prosciutto around the clock: "only the best for the best,
      Love, Frankie"—
there I was, rifling through the toiletry bags I kept in my
      carry-on.
For what? Never you mind. Nor had I bothered with
      breakfast . . .
How someone should have managed to remain unsettled like
      this
for decades now, such a case as would delight

the student of metempsychosis or literary biographer with a
   bent

for the pathological . . . I had had a home once, to be sure:

—*Aug, go and help Mom with groceries,*

                                   not unlike you . . .

SEMINAL VESTIBULE

I, too, found myself to be most at home there,
in this passageway between the street and . . . well,
let us say, the staircase and kingdom beyond
along with our Rottweiler pup Ondeen,
sprawled diagonally across the Afshar throw rug,
her belly rising and subsiding in wheezing, susurrant repose.
She might just as well have been a museum exhibit,
so nearly constant was her presence there
with me spread out on the little loveseat beside her,
stroking her ear between my fingers, teething on a stick of jerky
as was my custom in those days and sometimes even now
when circumstances and respite from society allow,
for it encourages, this chewing, deep memory to run off-leash,
sending me back once again to that antechamber
with its subaqueous lighting, yellow ochre walls, and doggie
    smell,
the old-fashioned tilted glass apothecary jars,
three each atop the twin console tables, Mother,
poor thing, between loads of wash, baking and polishing,
forever fussing to keep them aligned just so,
filled, as they were always kept, with jelly beans and candied
    fruit slices,
red, green, blue, black, and orange,
Poppa filled his pockets with, the fat fuck,
each time he wandered through between the one realm and
    t'other,

stepping over Ondeen, or not quite,
raising thus a grunt or high-pitched yelp of vivid pain.
How like a Kaiser Poppa could seem to be sometimes,
but gentle and loving, as well, pinching my cheek:
—*Now, don't be letting the world pass you by, sonny.*

A HISTORY OF WESTERN

MUSIC: CHAPTER 42

(Caspian Lake, Vermont)

Those French boys in the engine room aren't giving him much,
but he doesn't need much, does Carlos Wesley Byas of
    Muskogee, Oklahoma,
elbows on the bar at the Beaulieu, circa '47: —*I was born
    under the sign of music,*
he tells whoever's listening. That feathery tone of his by way of
    Hawk
but something else entirely, running through this set of ballads:
    "Laura,"
"Where or When," "Flamingo," unmistakable, no one played
    ballads like him.
Can't recall just where, Club Mephisto maybe, or the Vieux
    Colombier.
I've never seen the lake this still, Mt. Stannard across the way
    dissolving into mist,
then gone completely as night settles in, just as he's finishing up
    with "Stardust."
You can begin to make out a hint of bite in the air now, a couple
    of weeks
before you close the place down for the summer and head back
    to Boston,
or was it Brooklyn by then? I can't remember just when except
    it was delicious,

sitting there in the dark beside you, saying nothing, no need
for old friends
to say much of anything at all by this point, staring out into
the darkness,
finishing our drinks before heading back to the house for
dinner,
surely something wonderful, Beverly always had something
wonderful going.
Forgive me all this sentiment, but you were never one to shy
from sentiment
in your poems, the refined T'ang and Sung poets: *In my
younger days I*
*never / Tasted sorrow. I wanted / To become a famous poet. /
I wanted to get ahead /*
*So I pretended to be sad. / Now I am old and have tasted
every sorrow, /*
And I am content to loaf /And enjoy the clear autumn. [Hsin
Ch'i Chi] or Tu Fu's
"Restless Night" or "Full Moon," ever since you first read
Pound's *Cathay* at 19.
You'd always return to that well for refreshment, as have I, as
have I.
But we sit there awhile longer until the loons take up their
nocturnal chorus
as if on cue, almost directly on heels of night's arrival, and a
while after that.
This disc always tears me up whenever I play it, and I find it
nearly unbearable
not to be sharing it, sitting beside you at sunset, autumn
coming on.

S O

In memory of Michael O'Brien

So, my friend is gone,
whose counsel I depended on,
not in how I lived my life,
but in matters to do with language,
what words went where
or were best dispensed with entirely,
which, one might say, is less important
and more easily addressed.
So slender as to seem fragile,
he resembled an instrument
sensitive enough to register the slightest tremor
or shift in wind . . .
To whom do I turn for tuning now?

—*Sew buttons*, Mrs. Di Camillo, our neighbor next door
would reply when I'd turn up in her kitchen
and ask, as if on cue, "So?"
then give me a cookie,
for having played my part so well.
She must have sensed what was going on
across the rhododendrons. I loved her
and remember those cookies still.
She baked them herself, with colored sprinkles.
I remember her kindness

and the aroma of those cookies,
the most inviting haven of my young years.
Her kitchen was a place where I could go
should I ever have a need to sneak away.
Strange I should think of her now,
at this moment, 60 years later.
We would sing together, as well.
It only comes to me as I write this down,
and for the first time:
she must have had no children of her own.

"COMING ON THE HUDSON":

WEEHAWKEN

He seldom spoke, even when well, and when he did it was
    misterioso, brief,
a gnomic shorthand, often only a grunt,
but his musicians got it, Nellie, Boo-Boo, and Sphere III too.
Nowadays next to nothing comes out of his mouth, nothing at
    all.
—*What's with his head, Woo?*
(He insisted on calling all his doctors "Ping Pock Woo," can't
    say why.)
—*Dunno*, says Woo.
A Steinway, marooned, in a corner of the living room.
Him mostly in the bedroom. Nica's cats pad in and out,
licking themselves clean where they've collapsed in a puddle
    of sunshine.
Still, he carefully dresses every morning, spiffed up, suit and
    tie,
only to stay lying there in bed, glued to Bob Barker and *The
    Price Is Right*:
the dinette sets and double-door Amana refrigerators,
brought to you by 100% pure Dove soap and Imperial
    margarine.
Out the window of the old Von Sternberg house Nica's brother
    bought,
three Bauhaus cubes midst the frame & brick extravaganzas
    on Kings Bluff,

tugs push garbage scows south to the harbor's mouth and
open sea.

He watches the river all day long. That's what he does:

what the wind and light make of the water, for seasons on end,

the shimmer off the river at 9 a.m., the wakes the ferries and
cruise ships make—

headed where? Barbados? The Antilles? France?—

slowly passing across his field of vision like giant, ocean-going
wedding cakes.

What is there left to say, anyhow? Or play? They either got it
or not.

His world, or what of it that's stayed with him, lies directly
across the way:

the tenements of the old San Juan Hill neighborhood,
Minton's, 52nd Street—

none of it what it was, everything something else . . .

He watches as the lights begin to switch on across the river
come end of day,

the skyline and clouds above going electric with pinks and
reds

as the sun goes down behind him over the Meadowlands in the
west.

Sometimes at night, looking across, he feels a twinge, the
throb and pull of it.

But it don't pull all that hard, and it's too damn much of a
bother anyhow.

SHE

She was eating an onion as if it were an apple,
keeping her distance from the rest of us gathered there
on the shore of the vast and famous volcano lake.
It was an interlude for writers at some sort of literary affair.
We had just been served a dreadful local prosecco
the event's organizers seemed unreasonably proud of,
hick culture functionaries in this distant corner of Oceania.

Stand-offish though she may have affected to be,
I walked directly over to where she was standing and said,
—*Is the onion meant to discourage the plague of suitors*
who will be drawn like moths to the radiance of your beauty?
She barely acknowledged that I was even there, turning
her head ever so slightly in my direction as if she had picked
    out
in the breeze the faintest strains of an unfamiliar folk
    melody,

even though we had been lovers once, long ago,
passionately, memorably, including even murmurs of
    marriage.
She then turned herself further toward me, almost
    imperceptibly,
and said, in the chilly, rather formal manner of a chargé
    d'affaires
or barrister—*How deep do you suppose it is out there?*

Naturally, I wanted to fuck her. So, by the way, would you.
We could have hardly been farther from home, mine or hers,

with its bauxite-colored condo developments, shopping carts,
rows of garden hose nozzles set out like AK-47s at a gun show,
the two boys nearly grown now, her husband, a signal twerp
if ever there was one. My own circumstances will be of no real
    interest.
Still, she retained her remote, almost aristocratic demeanor.
—*600 feet or so*, I told her.
        Women, I find, can often behave quite strangely . . .

The black waters now filling the collapsed and empty magma
    chamber
stretched out before us. A great conflagration then suddenly
    lit up
a patch in the hills beyond, an explosion almost, a spectacle.
—*Fancy a swim?* I asked. The notion seemed to jar her
    insouciance,
if only slightly, but she turned to me now, fully, and drank
    me in,
wreck that I am, but with remnants . . . —*Why not*, she said,
and began to undress, only a few yards clear of the prosecco
    crew.

Her dainties, wet and clinging to her . . . Well, I had to catch
    my breath.
Likewise her skin and form, still both youthful and as I
    remembered.

A deep and most unusual sense of ease and delight welled
   up inside me
as she gracefully swam in tiny circles around me while I
   treaded water.
A magical zone, I could feel it, a holy place among the
   indigenous locals.
—*Tell me*, she said, swimming so close that now our bodies
   touched,
do you have an agent?

DRIVING BY BLUFF ROAD JUST

AFTER DUSK IN LATE AUTUMN

The house remains there still, almost hidden in shadow at
    the foot of the block,
the oaks and maples stripped of their leaves, atop the cliff,
the river 300 feet below, black waters trembling
as they recede from the rotted pilings at low tide, leaving
    behind a fetid wake.
The boy is in his room upstairs, second door on the right,
where he has always been, a bare Mazda bulb switched on
    in his head.
It's always on, this light, with a nimbus around it,
illuminating the big atlas he keeps at hand, lying open in
    bed beside him.
He riffles through it ceaselessly, like a supplicant fingering
    prayer beads.
He zooms in on every inlet, meadow, and lacustrine plain,
summoning them up as if in answer to some inner demand,
    stirring their surfaces
with his gaze, phosphors pooling at the bottom of each page.
He calls up great cities: Montevideos and Maharashtras,
entering through their gates at will, visiting their alleyways
    and boulevards,
the apothecaries, joss houses, and mills, unnoticed, as if a
    phantom,
drinking in every particular. To what end?

Even the most remote hill station and crumbling redoubt do
    not escape
his feverish attention, their contours and signs of
    weathering held up to the light.
Nothing must go unexamined, turned over and over,
    re-examined.
It seems that you, even with all your outward journeying,
    now find yourself lost,
while here the boy remains, attending to the work you long
    ago abandoned.

THE BENCH

What passed through your mind, old man,
what passed through your mind back then,
staring out beyond the shingle and sea wrack,
the islets and rocks,
to the Olympics on the far shore,
snowy peaks poking through cloud?

I would spot you often on this bench,
smoking your unfiltered Player's, gazing into the distance,
reading the grain of the sea,
the currents and wind,
as if parsing the whorls of Eadfrith's *Gospels*.
What can a young man—a boy, really—

know of what runs through an old man's mind?
But I wondered then, and wonder still,
no longer young, sitting here,
gazing as you once gazed at the patch of sea,
ever the same, ever changing,
the gulls and crows busily at work, hovering.

This sky would have been foreign to you,
the light, as well,
but not unpleasing, no, not at all—how could it be?—
swift-moving, full of drama,
weather and clouds rushing east overhead
until caught up in the coastal range,

and there unburdening themselves of their cargo.
It's fine light, at its best days like this,
almost pearly, a light mist.
I remember now, after so many years away,
how well it suits the place and suited me then, as now.
I stayed on for years.

But you moved along, and took the long way back,
by ship. You enjoyed the water,
watching it from this vantage or under you at sea.
You were the sort accustomed to moving on.
I spotted that about you straightaway.
You traveled light, the one book,

Njal's Saga, always in your left coat pocket.
Copper-wire moustache,
sea-reflecting eyes . . .
You'd long ago been a sailor yourself,
knowing what to take along, what leave behind.
There was more than a bit of the wanderer to you,

the exile, and in your carriage and gait:
no nonsense, erect, never inviting attention
but clearly not of this place.
I watched you carefully that year,
and listened.
It was good to be around a man like that.

One learns, takes in a great deal,
not even half-aware of it, not for many years later.
And not just how words join up,
made to fit properly together like the drystone walls
of a Yorkshire dale, sturdy, serviceable, lasting.
I watched you carefully that year.

That bungalow we'd meet at, the few of us,
rain pouring down outside,
listening to Scarlatti, Dowland, Byrd,
or you reading aloud to us, Wordsworth, Wyatt—
just back there across the road,
torn down, a gruesome condo complex now.

You poured those sounds into our heads.
Who knew what might come of it?
Surely, nothing bad.
I would walk past you many times that year,
sitting here, gazing out at the sea, the rocks.
Who can say what thoughts . . . ?

ACKNOWLEDGMENTS

The author wishes to thank the editors of the
London Review of Books, where most of these poems
first appeared, and also Hoboken Eddie's Mean Green
hot sauce for kick-starting these flights of fancy.